Exploring the World of Chemistry

by George Burns

illustrated by Nancy Woodman

A *Try This* Book
Franklin Watts
A Division of Grolier Publishing
New York ❀ London ❀ Hong Kong ❀ Sydney
Danbury, Connecticut

For Lisa
—George Burns

To my Dad, a chemist who
inspired my perpetual curiosity
—Nancy Woodman

Cover illustration by Nancy Woodman

Photographs copyright ©: Comstock, Inc.: pp. 6 (Bob Pizaro),
8 (George D. Lepp), 21 (R. Michael Stuckey); Photo Researchers, Inc.: pp. 15 (Patrick
Montagne), 26 (D.O.E./SS), 29 (Charles Falco/SS), 33, 38 (both Dr. Jeremy Burgess/SPL),
36 (Martin Land/SPL); Tom J. Ulrich: p. 17; Fundamental Photographs: pp. 24, 31 (both
Paul Silverman), 40 (Richard Megna).

Library of Congress Cataloging-in-Publication Data

Burns, George, 1952–
Exploring the world of chemistry / by George Burns;
illustrated by Nancy Woodman.
p. cm. — (Try this series)
Includes bibliographical references and index.
Summary: Suggests simple activities for exploring chemistry,
the study of the substances that make up our world.
ISBN 0-531-20119-8
1. Chemistry—Experiments—Juvenile literature. [1. Chemistry—Experiments
Juvenile literature. 2. Experiments.] I. Woodman, Nancy, ill. II. Title. III. Series.
QD38.B87 1995
540'.78—dc20

95-9537
CIP AC

CONTENTS

THE WORLD OF CHEMISTRY

Have you ever really thought about what happens when you bake a cake? You mix together some flour, sugar, eggs, yeast, and milk. You put it in a hot oven and watch it rise. When it's done, your pan is bursting with a solid cake. How did this light, spongy stuff come from a few powders and liquids?

Many other amazing things take place during cooking. Have you noticed that when water boils, it disappears? What happens to it?

How about cooking outside on a charcoal grill? Why does the charcoal burn? Why does it glow red with flame and then turn into gray ashes?

If you have ever asked yourself questions like these, then you have already taken your first steps toward becoming a *chemist*. (To learn how to pronounce any word in italics, look it up in the glossary at the back of the book.)

Chemistry is the study of the substances that make up everything around us. They include the water we

Chemists explore how substances like oil and water interact.

drink, the air we breathe, the clothes we wear, and the ground we walk on. All of these are called *matter*.

Chemists study matter. They want to know what it's made of, how it acts, and how it changes. They can tell you why your soda pop fizzes when it is poured. And why oil and water don't mix. They can even tell you why things burn.

Chemists like to combine different substances called *chemicals*. Then they watch to see what happens. Sometimes, as if by magic, the chemicals turn into something that looks completely different. And they may sizzle or even explode when they do it! Chemists know a lot about how substances react with each other.

It is no wonder they sometimes seem like magicians.

In this book, you can be a chemist and explore the matter you find in your own home. You will learn to start thinking like a real chemist.

One thing professional chemists do is keep careful records of their work. You may want to get a notebook or pad to keep track of all the things you do in these activities. Be a chemist and try these activities!

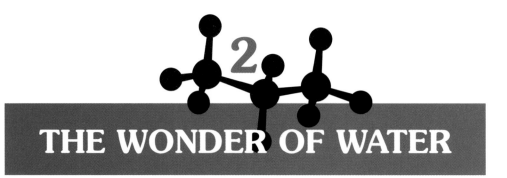

THE WONDER OF WATER

What if you asked for water and someone handed you an ice cube? You might think it was a joke. But an ice cube is made of water. It is water that has been frozen. Chemists would say that ice is water in its *solid* form.

Ice is water that has been frozen.

Water, like all matter, can exist in three forms: *solid*, *liquid*, and *gas*. When is water a liquid? Water is a liquid when it's running freely from the tap, being poured from a glass, falling from the sky as rain, or flowing in a stream. Do you know when water might be a gas? If not, you will soon find out.

Chemists call these three forms *states* of water. You can see all the different states of water by doing the following activities.

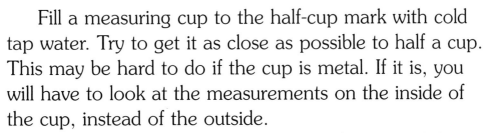

Try This:

Fill a measuring cup to the half-cup mark with cold tap water. Try to get it as close as possible to half a cup. This may be hard to do if the cup is metal. If it is, you will have to look at the measurements on the inside of the cup, instead of the outside.

Place your half cup of water in the freezer. While you have the freezer door open, put a metal baking pan in there, too. You will need a cold metal pan later. Write down the time you put the cup of water in the freezer. How long do you think it will take the water to freeze? Write down your guess.

Check every fifteen minutes or so to see whether the water has frozen. Open the door just a crack, but don't leave it open too long. Otherwise, the cold air will escape. That could change the time it takes your water to freeze.

When you are sure that the water is completely solid, write down the time. How long did it take to freeze? What made the water freeze?

It's cold in the freezer. The water froze because its temperature dropped.

Take the cup out of the freezer. How much solid water is in the cup? Is it still half a cup? Why do you think it measures the amount it does? Put the cup back in the freezer for now.

Did you find more water in your cup after it froze? You may have seen only a bulge or a crack on the surface of the water. That's because water *expands* when it changes from liquid to solid. It actually grows larger. Most substances do just the opposite. They *contract*, or shrink, when they become solid. Water is one of the few that doesn't. Even though it is *everywhere*, it is one of the most unusual substances on earth.

Have you ever seen a glass bottle break in the freezer? That happens when the freezing water inside the bottle expands so much that the glass breaks. Juices and milk can do this too, because they contain water. Did you know that water was so powerful?

Now fill a second measuring cup to the half-cup mark with hot tap water. Make sure the water is not too hot or you could burn yourself. Put this second cup in the freezer, too. Write down the time.

Think about how long it took the first cup of water to freeze. How long do you think it will take this second cup of water to turn to ice? Write down your guess.

As you did before, check the cup to see when the water has frozen. When it is ice, write down the time. Which cup took longer to freeze? Why do you think this is so?

Suppose you wanted the frozen water to turn back into a liquid. How could you get it to do that?

You would have to raise its temperature. This time leave the cup out on a counter or table where it won't be disturbed. Write down the time again. How long do you think it will take to turn back into a liquid?

When your cup once again is all liquid water instead of ice, write down the time. How long did it take the water to change states? Was it about the same amount of time as it took to turn solid? Look at the measurement again. How much liquid water is in the cup now? Why do you think that is?

It's a Gas

What do you think will change the water to a gas? If you left the cup on the counter for a long time, the water would change into a gas all by itself. But you can change the temperature more quickly to help it along.

Try This:

You will need to use the stove for this activity. Ask an adult's permission before you start, and have an adult watch as you do the activity.

Pour the cup of water from the previous activity into a pot. Set the pot over medium heat on the stove. As the pot heats up, water begins to rise out of the pot. You can't see the water because it's in the

13

form of an invisible gas called *water vapor*. To make sure that the water vapor is really there, take the metal pan out of the freezer (from the first activity). Hold it upside down about a foot over the pot of water.

After a few minutes, take a look at the inside of the pan. Is it covered with liquid water? When the water vapor hits the cold pan, the change in temperature changes it back into its liquid state.

Make sure you turn off the stove and clean up any water that has spilled. Put away the pot, pan, and cup.

When matter is in its solid state, the space it takes up doesn't change. Another word for this space is *volume*.

You measured a certain volume of ice in your cup. If you had dumped the ice out of the cup, the ice would still take up the same volume. And it would keep the same shape.

When matter is in its liquid state, it takes the shape of whatever is holding it. If you had poured your water

This geyser in Yellowstone National Park is giving off water vapor, or steam.

into a skinnier measuring cup or dumped it on the table, the water would have had a different shape. But the amount of water would not have changed. The volume of water would still be half a cup.

When matter is in the form of a gas, it doesn't take up any particular amount of space. It spreads out into whatever space is there. The water vapor that rose from your pot spread out into the air in your kitchen. Because of this, you could not measure the volume of the water vapor.

Gases don't have any particular shape, either. This is difficult for us to see because most gases are invisible. They float through the air in many different shapes. If they are inside a closed container, they take the shape of the container.

Try This:

Leave a half cup of water out on a counter or on a shelf. After several days, see how much water is in the cup. Water will slowly change into a gas at room temperature. When liquid water turns into water vapor, chemists say the water is *evaporating*.

Try This:

Look around your house. Make a list of different things you find. Write down whether each object or substance is a solid, a liquid, or a gas.

3

THE MYSTERY OF GASES

We can't see it, but the most common gas around us is air. Air is actually made of a number of different gases: *oxygen*, *nitrogen*, *carbon dioxide*, and *argon*. Oxygen is the gas our bodies need to live. It's what our lungs take out of the air as we breathe.

Porpoises come to the surface for oxygen.

But if you can't see oxygen, how can you tell it's there? How could you tell whether you were walking into a room full of air or a room full of some other kind of gas that you couldn't breathe?

Try This:

Since you will need to use matches for this activity, ask a grown-up's permission to do it before you start. It may be helpful to have a grown-up watch while you do the activity.

You will need to stand a short candle in a pan of water. A short, fat candle between 2 and 2 1/2 inches (5 to 6 cm) high works best. You will also be turning a jar upside down over the candle. Get a narrow jar, such as an olive jar, about 6 to 8 inches (15 to 20 cm) high. Make sure it is large enough to fit over the candle.

If your candle is too narrow to stand in a pan, put it in a very small candle holder or a bottle cap.

Clear off a table so you have room to work. Now put about 1/2 inch (1 cm) of water in a cooking pan and set it on the table. Add a few drops of food coloring, if you have it. It will help you see what's happening better.

Put the candle in the pan and place the jar over it so that the rim of the jar rests on the bottom of the pan. Mark the level of the water on the jar with a marker. Remove the jar and light the candle. Just before putting the jar back over the candle, write down the position of

the second hand on a clock or watch. Carefully put the jar over the candle as it was before. Watch what happens.

When the flame on the candle goes out, write down the time in seconds. Why did the flame go out?

The flame needs oxygen to burn. There was some oxygen in the air that you trapped above the water in the jar. But no more oxygen could get in. When the flame used up all the oxygen inside the jar, the candle went out.

You might think of the flame as being suffocated. People suffocate when they don't have oxygen to breathe.

Does the air in the jar look any different now? Since all the gases in air are invisible, we can't even tell that there is no oxygen left. But what happened to the water level inside the jar? As the flame took oxygen from the air, the air took up less space. The water rose higher to fill the space that the oxygen left empty.

You don't have to worry about walking into a room with no air in it. But you do have to be very careful that you don't put anything over your head that won't let air in. Also, don't climb into small, closed spaces where there's not much air. You could use up all the oxygen just like the flame.

The Gases You Breathe

Take a deep breath. Then blow it out on your hand. Does your breath feel warm? What exactly did you suck into your lungs? What did you blow out?

As we said before, your lungs take oxygen out of the air. They deliver it to the blood so that oxygen can spread all over your body. All the cells in your body need oxygen to live.

Lungs also remove carbon dioxide from the blood. You exhaled carbon dioxide and other gases into the air. Your breath feels warm because your body warms up the gases. Your body temperature is about 98.6° F (37° C).

This girl is exhaling bubbles of a gas called carbon dioxide.

Try This:

Blow up a balloon, but don't tie it. Pinch it closed with your thumb and finger. What's inside the balloon? Most people would say it's filled with air. But to be more exact, it's filled with the carbon dioxide and other gases you exhaled into the balloon.

Release your thumb and finger while holding onto the balloon with your other hand. Put your free hand in front of the opening of the balloon. Did all the carbon dioxide come out? Did you hear it? Did you see it? Did you feel it? Why didn't it stay in the balloon?

The balloon squeezed the carbon dioxide gas out of the balloon. You probably heard the open end of the balloon vibrating as the gas rushed by. You could not see the gas itself. But you could see its effect on the balloon. And you should have been able to feel it on your hand.

Try This:

Fill up the sink with water. Blow up a balloon less than halfway and pinch it closed. Hold the balloon under the water. Why is it hard to keep the balloon down? What do you think would happen if you let the gas out under water?

Let the gas out of the balloon and see if you were right. Did you see bubbles of carbon dioxide float up

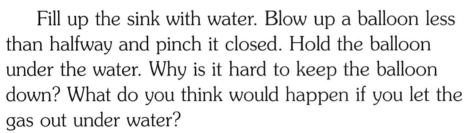

through the water? You may think you are seeing the carbon dioxide itself. But you are really only seeing the space the gas makes in the water. The gas itself is invisible.

Why didn't the gas stay in the water? Why did it rise up into the air? Because carbon dioxide is lighter than water. That's why it is hard to keep the balloon under water.

Try This:

You will need two bottles of seltzer or soda water for this activity. You will also need two large balloons. Keep one bottle cold in the refrigerator. Let the other sit out for a while until it is warm.

Do this activity outside or over a sink because it could spray water. Carefully open the cold seltzer bottle. Open it a little and then close it right away a few times. That way it won't squirt all over. Then stretch the opening of a balloon over the top of the open bottle. Hold the balloon so that it doesn't slip off the top of the bottle. Then watch what happens.

Seltzer and sodas are *carbonated*. That means carbon dioxide has been added to them. You can see tiny bubbles of the gas when sodas fizz. The bubbles give soda an extra zing in your mouth.

When you open a bottle of seltzer, the gas starts rushing out. If the bottle was shaken, the gas may have built up in the space at the top of the bottle. Then it rushes out faster and pulls some of the water with it.

Bubbles of carbon dioxide rise in water

With the cap off, the carbon dioxide has someplace to go, so more of it rises out of the liquid. You should have seen your balloon filling up with this rising gas. It fills the balloon just like your breath does. Try shaking the bottle a little. The gas will leave the liquid faster. Your balloon should fill even more.

Now, with your second balloon ready, quickly open the warm bottle of seltzer. Immediately slip the balloon over the top of the bottle. Watch as the balloon fills with carbon dioxide. Which of your two balloons grew the largest? The one over the cold bottle or the one over the warm bottle? Why do you think that happened?

Carbon dioxide mixes more easily with cold liquids. It rises faster in warm liquids. So less carbon dioxide came out of the cold bottle than the warm bottle.

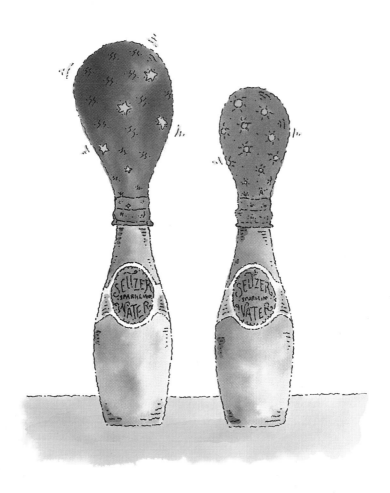

To see what happens when seltzer gets really hot, get another bottle of cold seltzer. Open it and put a cork into the top of it. Set it in the hot sun away from people and animals. As the seltzer heats up, the carbon dioxide will keep rising out of the liquid. It will push so hard that the cork should eventually pop right out of the bottle.

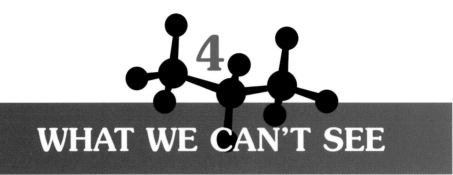

WHAT WE CAN'T SEE

If ice, water, and water vapor look and act so differently, what is it that makes them water? It is something in them that we can't see, but chemists know is there. Inside water are tiny particles called *atoms*.

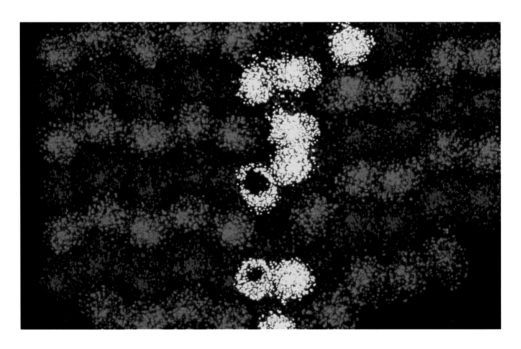

Powerful microscopes let us see atoms in materials.

Atoms are inside all matter. Some substances have only one kind of atom. Chemists call them *elements*. Oxygen is an element because it is made of only oxygen atoms. *Hydrogen* is another element. Water has both oxygen and hydrogen atoms in it. Because it has more than one kind of atom, chemists call water a *compound*.

The oxygen and hydrogen atoms join together in small groups called *molecules*. There are two hydrogen atoms and one oxygen atom in a water molecule. This molecule is the tiniest piece of water there is. The same molecule is repeated over and over again to make water that you can see. Water vapor and ice have the same molecule inside them. That's why they're water, too.

You can make a molecule you can see from modeling clay.

Try This:

First try making a water molecule. To make the oxygen atom, roll some modeling clay into a ball about 1/2 inch (1 cm) wide. Use a different color clay to make two hydrogen atoms. Roll out two balls that are slightly smaller than the oxygen atom.

Connect the atoms with toothpicks that have been

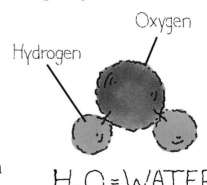

$H_2O = WATER$

broken in half. If you want to, you can connect them with used wooden matchsticks instead. Put a hydrogen atom on either side of the oxygen atom so that they all form a V shape. Now you have a water molecule. Chemists call it H_2O to show that it has two hydrogen atoms and one oxygen atom.

Now make more molecules of water. Put them next to each other to show how they build up in water. If you want to make water vapor, leave a lot of space between the molecules. When water evaporates, the molecules move farther away from each other. The extra heat gives them energy to bounce around faster. So they go into the air where they have more room to move.

When the temperature lowers, the molecules move closer together as they slow down. But as you saw in the first activity, something unusual happens if it gets cold enough for the water to turn to ice. The molecules move farther apart as they freeze. So the molecules of ice should be slightly farther apart than the molecules of liquid water.

You can make models of other molecules, too. Carbon dioxide, the gas that we exhale, has one carbon atom

Carbon

Oxygen

CO_2 = CARBON DIOXIDE

and two oxygen atoms in its molecule. Make the carbon atom slightly larger than the oxygen atoms. With toothpicks, stick each oxygen atom on either side of the carbon atom in a straight line. Chemists call carbon dioxide CO_2.

Salt is made of elements called *sodium* and *chlorine*. An atom of sodium and an atom of chlorine are repeated over and over again in a cube shape.

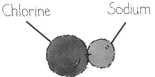

Chlorine   Sodium

NaCl = Salt

Make a small sodium atom out of one color of modeling clay. Make the chlorine atom about twice as large from a different color clay. Stick them together with a toothpick. Make many of these pairs and build them into a cube with toothpicks.

Salt Crystal

called a salt crystal. Try looking at a salt crystal under a magnifying glass. You will see that it is actually a cube shape. Sugar and other solids

When atoms line up in this way, they can create beautiful solids called *crystals*. The smooth faces of the cube reflect light and make it sparkle. A grain of salt is

Grains of salt are actually tiny cubes.

form crystals, too. You will learn more about crystals in upcoming activities.

Mixing It Up

Chemists like to study how things mix together. Have you noticed that the way liquids mix with each other is very different from the way solids mix?

Think about playing a game of checkers. What's the first thing you do after you open up the board? You usually divide up the checkers. One person gathers the black pieces and the other gathers the red pieces. Even if the checkers are all mixed up, it doesn't take long to separate them. That's because checkers are solid.

Liquids mix much more closely than solids do. The molecules of different liquids flow around each other. Because of this, they are much more difficult to separate than solids.

Try This: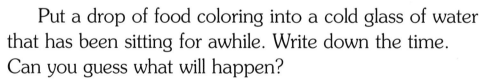

Put a drop of food coloring into a cold glass of water that has been sitting for awhile. Write down the time. Can you guess what will happen?

Watch carefully as the food coloring moves through the water. How long does it take before the water is all the same color? Write down the time.

The molecules of water in the glass are constantly moving. But we don't notice that until the food coloring is added. Molecules of liquid food coloring spread out evenly

throughout the water. They slip in between the molecules of water. Soon you get a very complete mixture of food coloring and water. What happens if you add more drops of food coloring to the water?

Now put a drop of food coloring into a very warm glass of water. Write down the time. What do you think will happen?

Watch carefully as the food coloring moves through the water. How long does it take before the water is all the same color? Write down the time.

Which glass of water took longer to become all the same color? Molecules

When liquids mix, their molecules slide around each other.

of warm water move much faster than molecules of cold water. That is why the molecules of food coloring spread more quickly through the glass of warm water.

What if you wanted to separate the food coloring from the water? How would you do it?

If you had a mixture of sugar and salt crystals, you might be able to separate them. It would take a lot of time, but you could do it. You could separate them crystal by crystal, using a magnifying glass to tell them apart. But if you want to separate your two liquids, you have to give up the water to do it.

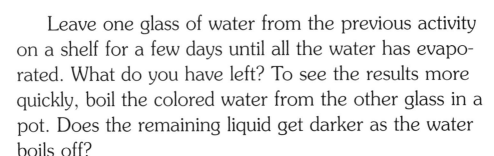

Try This:

Leave one glass of water from the previous activity on a shelf for a few days until all the water has evaporated. What do you have left? To see the results more quickly, boil the colored water from the other glass in a pot. Does the remaining liquid get darker as the water boils off?

Some liquids don't mix as well as others. Can you think of any?

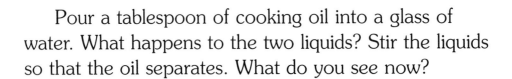

Try This:

Pour a tablespoon of cooking oil into a glass of water. What happens to the two liquids? Stir the liquids so that the oil separates. What do you see now?

oil

water

Let the glass of liquids sit for a while. What happens? Do the two liquids ever mix?

Oil and water just don't mix. Oil is much lighter than water so it floats on top. Oil and vinegar don't mix very well either. That's why you often see people shaking their salad dressing bottles before pouring.

Look at an oil-and-vinegar salad dressing that has been sitting on the shelf for a while. You should be able to see two separate layers—one of vinegar, one of oil.

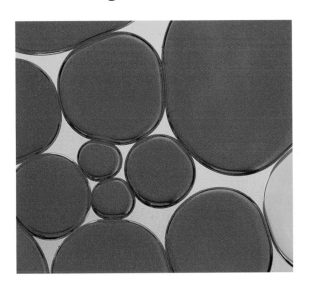

These red, purple, and orange drops of water will not mix with the yellow oil.

33

Crystals in Your Cup

Have you ever been told not to drink too much soda because there's a lot of sugar in it? But where's the sugar in a glass of soda? You can taste it, but can you see it?

Sugar is a solid made of small crystals. But when it's added to liquid, something happens to it. It becomes a special kind of a mixture called a *solution*.

Try This:

Put one teaspoon of sugar into a glass of water. Mix the sugar and water. Can you see the sugar in the water? Take a sip of the water. Can you taste the sugar?

Put another teaspoon of sugar in the glass and stir. Can you see the sugar now? How does it taste?

Continue to add teaspoons of sugar one at a time. Keep track of how many teaspoons you add to the water. Make sure you stir the water after each teaspoon, and wait a minute before adding the next one. Stop adding sugar when you see sugar collecting at the bottom of the glass. How many teaspoons of sugar do you think you can add?

Was your guess right? When you stirred in the first spoonfuls of sugar, you couldn't see it. Why is the sugar starting to collect on the bottom now?

When sugar mixes with water, it *dissolves* in the water. The sugar crystals mix so closely with the molecules of water that you can't see them. But you can taste the sweetness of the sugar in the water.

Water can dissolve only so much sugar. When it has dissolved as much as it can, chemists say the water is *saturated*. Any solution can become saturated when too much solid is added.

Leave your solution of sugar water in a place where it won't be disturbed. After all the water has evaporated, what do you have left? Measure the sugar left in the glass to see if it's the same amount you put in.

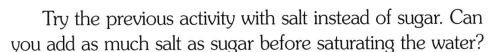

Try This:

Try the previous activity with salt instead of sugar. Can you add as much salt as sugar before saturating the water?

Now try adding salt to a glass of hot water. Can you put more teaspoons of salt in cold water or hot water?

Do all solids dissolve in water? Try dissolving a teaspoon of sand in water.

Sand is too heavy to dissolve in water. It sinks right to the bottom of the glass. That's why it sinks to the bottom of the ocean, too. Other solids are too light to dissolve in water. Dust, for example, floats on top of the water.

There are many kinds of crystals other than salt and sugar. Crystals form in solid materials, including ice and snow. Rocks, such as quartz and diamonds, can be crystals, too. You can grow your own crystals in the next activity.

These are crystals of a kind of quartz, a mineral found underground.

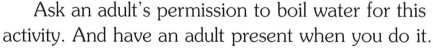

Try This:

Ask an adult's permission to boil water for this activity. And have an adult present when you do it.

Get a long pencil, a paper clip, and some string. Tie one end of the string to the middle of the pencil. Tie a paper clip to the string about 6 inches (9 cm) away from the pencil. Place the clip in a large ceramic coffee cup and rest the pencil across the top. Make sure you don't use a glass cup because it could break.

Pour one cup of water into a cooking pot and bring it to a boil. Measure two cups of sugar while waiting for the water to boil. When it is boiling, *sterilize* the clip and the string. Holding onto one end of the pencil, dip the clip and some of the string into the water near the edge of the pot. Hold it there for about 15 seconds. This will kill any germs on the clip. Then put the clip back into the coffee cup.

Measure two cups of sugar. Stir all the sugar into the boiling water until it completely dissolves. Turn off the heat and carefully pour the sugar water into your coffee cup.

Position the pencil across the cup so that the paper clip hangs down into the middle of the sugar water solution. Roll the string around the pencil until the clip is not touching the bottom of the cup.

Leave the cup in a place where it won't be disturbed.

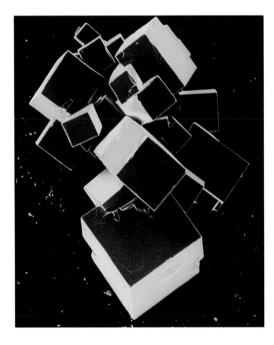

As a crystal of salt grows, cubes build on top of each other.

Now all you have to do is watch the crystals grow! The longer you let the water sit, the larger the crystals will grow. If a layer of crystals covers the water, carefully spoon them off.

You have just made rock candy. It is all right to taste it, since you

sterilized the string and paper clip beforehand. The crystals may not be as precious as diamonds, but they should be sweeter.

38

5

EXPLORING CHEMICALS

Many people think chemicals are strange or dangerous substances found in a laboratory. But we come into contact with chemicals every day. They are the substances that make up everything around us. Water, sugar, salt, and carbon dioxide are all chemicals.

The sweetness in our food is usually caused by some form of sugar. Sometimes it is caused by chemicals that substitute for sugar. But when things taste sour, it is probably because of an *acid*.

An acid is a chemical compound that has hydrogen and other elements in it. Orange juice and lemonade have acids in them. That's why they have a sour taste. Many foods contain acids. So does your body.

But some acids are so powerful that they can burn right through skin. Don't ever touch anything labeled as an acid unless you know what it is.

Foods that taste bitter probably have a *base* in them. Bases are chemical compounds that can be very powerful like acids. That is why they are often found in cleaning

A strong acid can eat right through a penny.

products. But bases are, in a way, the opposite of acids. When you mix an acid with a base, they take the strength away from each other. A chemist would say that they *neutralize* each other.

How would you find out if an unknown liquid is an acid or a base? You would never want to taste it because it could be harmful. But you could give it a color test. Chemists dip *litmus paper* into liquids and see what color the paper turns. The color tells them whether the liquid is an acid or a base. You can do a similar test using the cooking water from red cabbage.

Try This:

Ask an adult for permission to use the stove. And have an adult watch while you are cooking. Cut a wedge of red cabbage into small pieces. Put two cups of water and the cabbage into a cooking pot. Cook it over low heat for about twenty minutes.

Let the cabbage water cool. Set out three or four cups in a row. When the water has cooled, pour it into the cups. Throw the cabbage out—or eat it if you like.

Now you are ready to do some testing. In your notebook, make a chart like the one below.

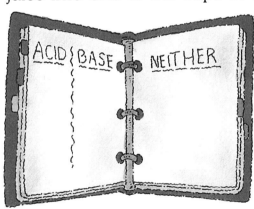

Try putting a spoonful of lemon juice into one of the cups of cabbage juice. It should turn pinkish. That's because lemon juice has acid in it. Acids cause the cabbage water to turn pink. List lemon juice under "Acid" in your chart. Put the pink cup of cabbage juice aside. You might want to label it "lemon juice" so you don't mix it up with the other cups.

Add a spoonful of baking soda to a different cup of cabbage juice. The cabbage juice should turn green. That's because baking soda is a base. Bases turn the

cabbage water green. List baking soda under "Base" in your chart.

Now test other substances you find in your refrigerator or around your house. Some interesting things to

test are other juices, coffee, tea, milk, cleaning liquid, vinegar, cream of tartar, and soda. Each time you test something, use a new cup of cabbage juice. You can always make more juice if you need it.

List each substance you try in one of the columns in your notebook. If the cabbage water does not turn pink or green, list the substance under "Neither." After you have tested several substances, compare the colors the cabbage juice has turned. You will find that stronger acids turn the water a lighter pink. Stronger bases turn the water a darker green.

In the activities in this book, you have explored some common chemicals. Now that you have had some experience as a chemist, start investigating other chemicals. How many chemicals can you find listed as ingredients on food products in your home? You might find *ferrous sulfate*, *zinc oxide*, or *folic acid*. They may sound scary, but they are just minerals and vitamins that help you stay healthy.

If you see an ingredient that is in a lot of foods, try to find information on it at the library.

Also look at the ingredients on cleaning products. When you or someone else uses a cleanser, make observations about it. How does it change as it is used? Write your observations in your notebook.

If you want to try mixing some substances, make sure you get an adult's approval first. Record in your notebook anything you observe about how the chemicals change. Also, write down any questions you have and any new information you discover.

You will find that chemistry does not happen only in a laboratory. It is happening around us all the time. You just have to keep your eyes open and experiment!

GLOSSARY

acid (ASS-id)—a type of chemical that tastes sour. Strong acids can burn through substances, even skin. Acids neutralize bases.

argon (AR-gon)—one of the invisible gases in air.

atom (AT-um)—a tiny particle that is the basic building block of all matter. It is the smallest piece of an element.

base—a type of chemical that tastes bitter. Bases neutralize acids.

carbon dioxide (KAR-bun die-OX-ide)—one of the gases in air. People and animals exhale carbon dioxide. Plants take it in through their pores.

carbonated (KAR-bun-ate-ed)—containing carbon dioxide bubbles, as a liquid like soda does.

chemical (KEM-i-kull)—a substance that a chemist studies. It is usually an element or a compound.

chemist (KEM-ist)—a scientist who studies the materials that make up everything on earth.

chemistry (KEM-is-tree)—the study of materials and how they react with each other. It includes what materials are made of, how they behave, and how they change.

chlorine (KLOR-een)—an element in table salt. It is also added to water in swimming pools.

compound (KOM-pound)—a substance made of two or more elements. Compounds form when the atoms of different elements bond together in molecules.

contract (kon-TRAKT)—to get smaller; to decrease in volume.

crystal (KRIS-tull)—a solid in which the atoms are arranged in cubes. The smooth faces of the cubes cause them to sparkle.

dissolve (dih-ZOLV)—to mix and melt with a liquid until invisible. Solids dissolve in liquids in solutions.

element (ELL-uh-ment)—a substance containing only one kind of atom. It is one of the basic materials that make up everything on earth.

evaporate (ih-VAP-uh-rate)—to boil away; to change from a liquid to a gas.

expand (ik-SPAND)—to get larger; to increase in volume.

ferrous sulfate (FERR-us SULL-fate)—a mineral containing iron.

folic acid (FOE-lick ASS-id)—a chemical that is one of the B vitamins.

gas—the airlike form of a substance. It occurs at temperatures higher than the boiling point.

hydrogen (HI-droh-jen)—an element that combines with oxygen to make water.

liquid (LICK-wid)—the flowing form of a substance. Its temperature must be higher than the melting point but lower than the boiling point.

litmus (LIT-muss) paper—paper that chemists dip in chemicals to find out whether they are acids or bases. The color the paper turns shows how acidic or basic the chemical is.

matter (MAT-ter)—anything that occupies space; any material that has weight.

molecule (MOLL-uh-kyule)—a group of atoms bonded together. It is the basic building block of compounds, or the smallest piece of a compound.

neutralize (NOO-trah-lize)—to make neither acidic nor basic; to counteract the effect of an acid with a base or vice versa.

nitrogen (NIE-troh-jen)—one of the gases in air. Air is made mostly of nitrogen.

oxygen (OX-uh-jen)—one of the gases in air. People and animals inhale oxygen. They need it to live. Plants give off oxygen. Oxygen also combines with hydrogen to make water.

quartz (kworts)—a kind of mineral, or rock, that is made of crystals.

saturate (SATCH-uh-rate)—to dissolve as much solid as possible in a liquid.

sodium (SOH-dee-um)—an element in table salt.

solid (SOLL-id)—the hard form of a substance. It exists when the temperature is lower than the melting point.

solution (suh-LOO-shun)—a mixture of a liquid and a solid.

states (states)—the three forms a substance can take. They are solid, liquid, and gas.

sterilize (STER-uh-lize)—to kill or remove germs.

volume (VOL-yume)—an amount of space. The volume of a substance is the amount of space it occupies.

water vapor (WAH-ter VAY-per)—water that has evaporated. In this state, water is a gas.

zinc oxide (zink OX-ide)—a mineral containing zinc and oxygen. It is found in medicines and ointments.

INDEX

Page numbers in *italics* indicate illustrations.